Light Armoured Draisine TK

(TK light armoured track and all-terrain draisine)

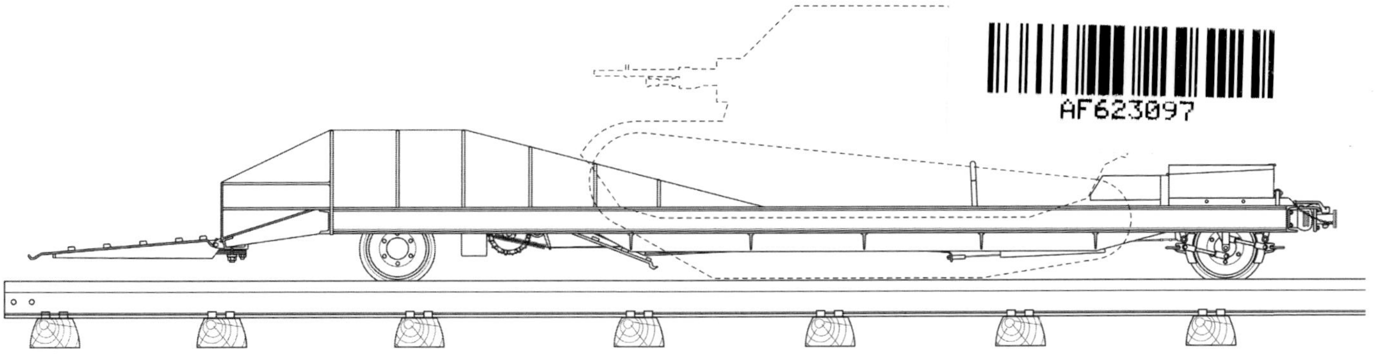

TK rail track guide (early type, view from left, the dotted line shows the TK-3 tank in position "for self-driving").

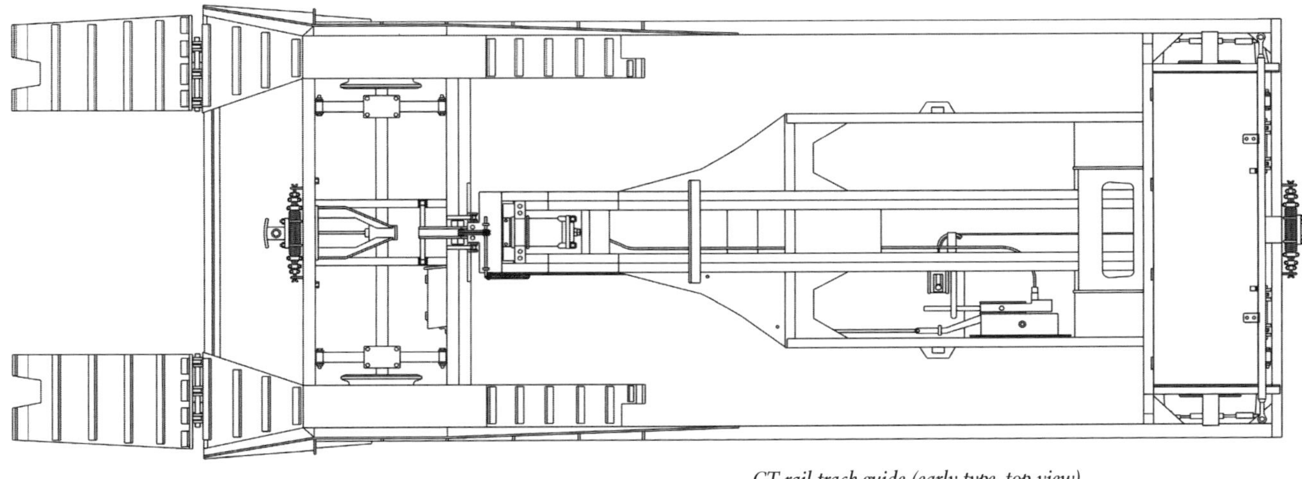

CT rail track guide (early type, top view).

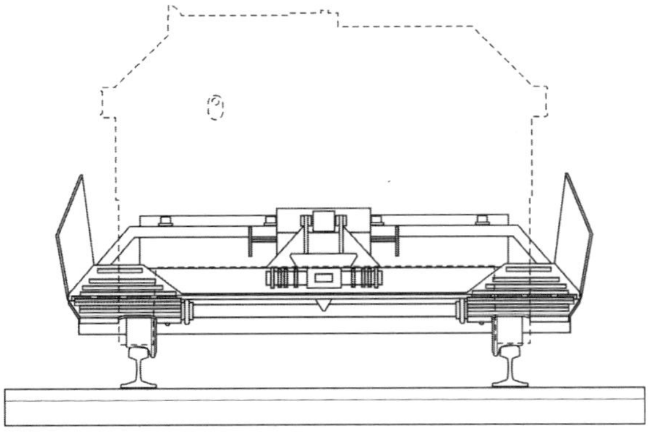

TK rail track guide (early type, front view, girder lowered – in lower position, dashed line shows the TK-3 tank in the 'free-running' position).

TK rail track guide (later type, reinforced, view from left, dashed line shows girder in lower position, changed front of entry side wings).

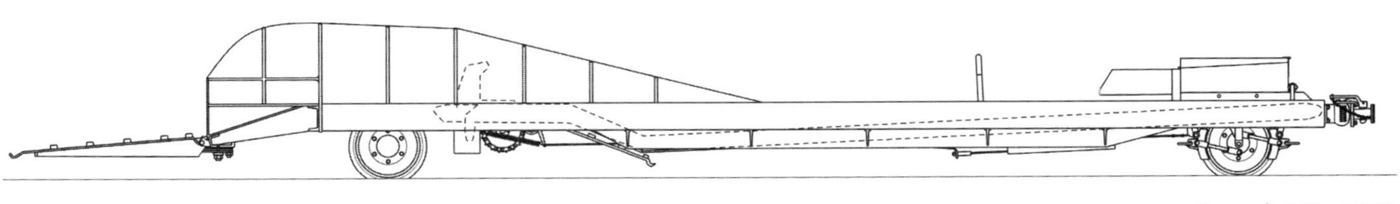

1/35

Drawings: Adam Jońca

TK-3 tankette from the draisines platoon of the Polish armoured train

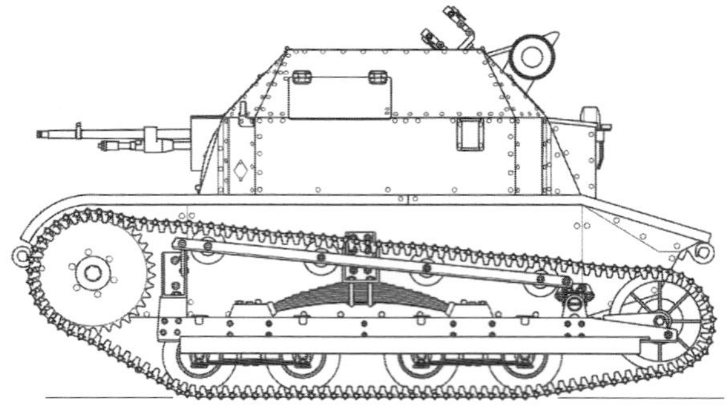

A standard TK-3 tankette from the armoured train's draisine platoon (left-hand view, extension pads in place.).

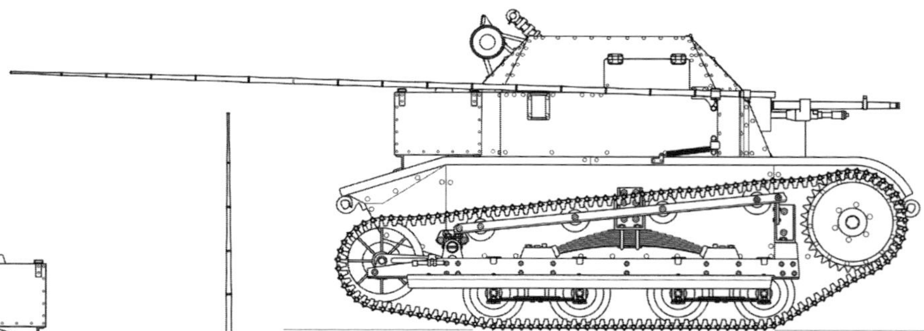

TK-3 tankette with radio station (view from right, antenna mast laid 'to march', external prop boxes and extension caps added).

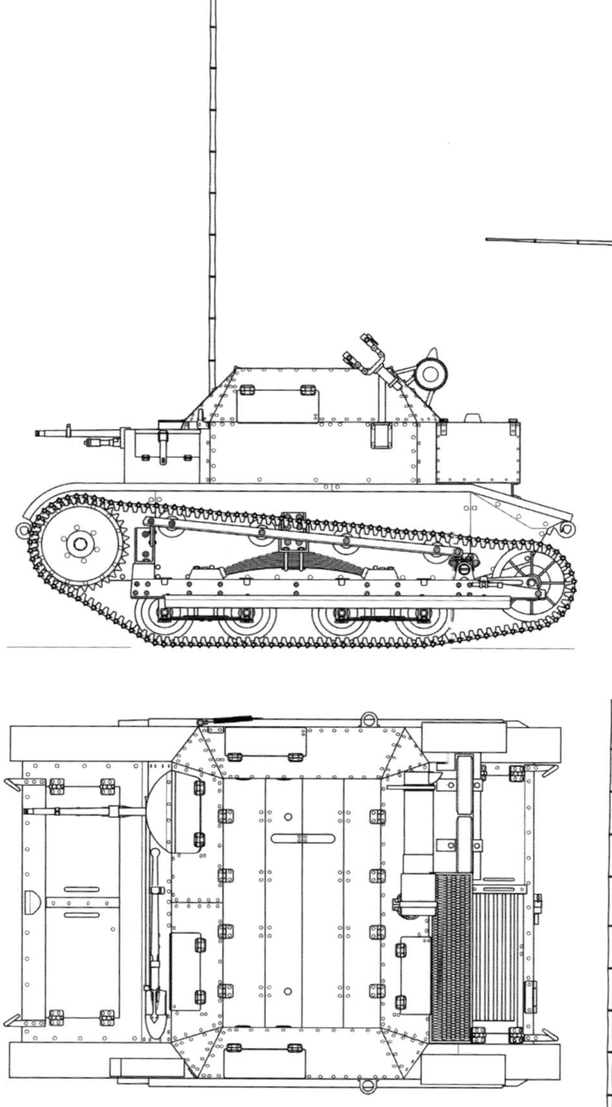

TK-3 tankette with radio station (left view and top view).

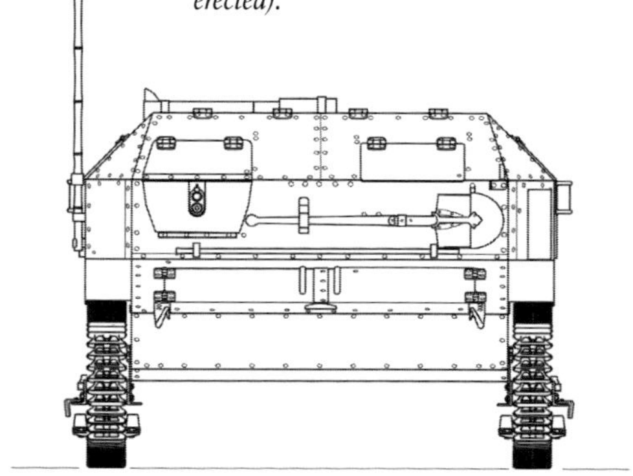

TK-3 tankette with radio station (front view, antenna mast erected).

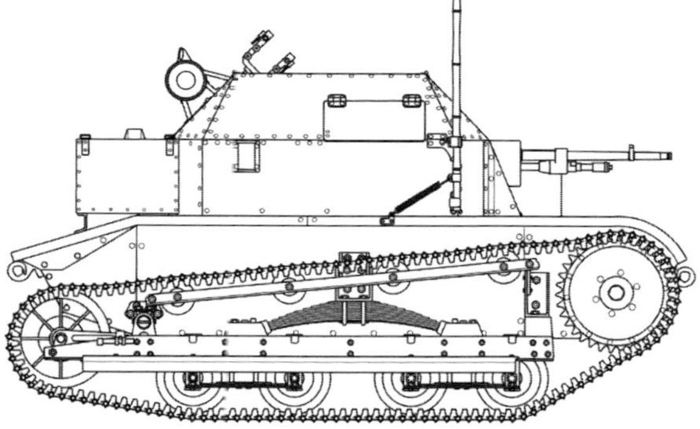

TK-3 tankette with radio station (right-hand view, antenna mast erected).

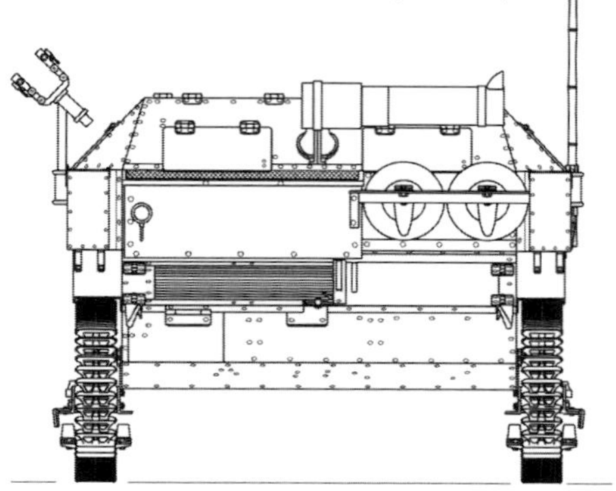

TK-3 tankette with radio station (rear view).

1/35

Drawings: Adam Jońca

TKS tankette from the draisines platoon of the Polish armoured train

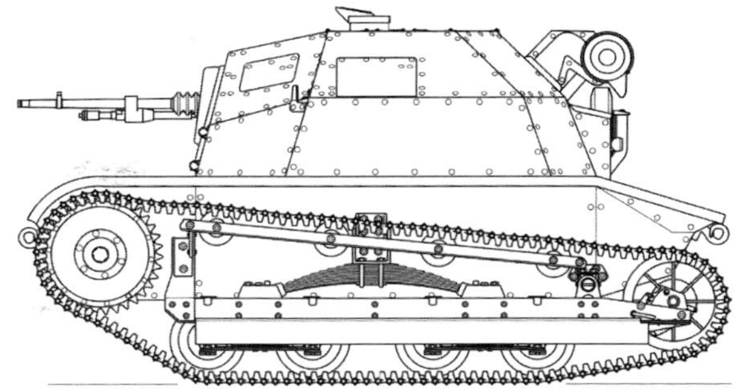

A standard TKS tankette from the armoured train derrick platoon (left-hand view, extension pads fitted).

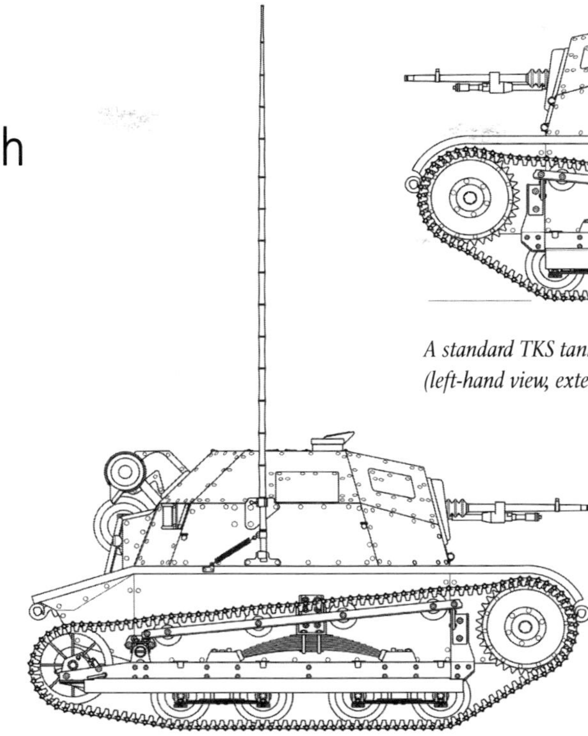

TKS tankette with radio station (right-hand view, antenna mast erected).

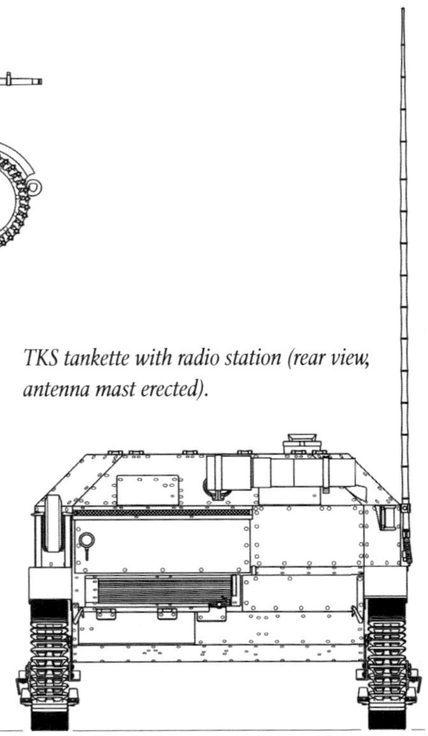

TKS tankette with radio station (rear view, antenna mast erected).

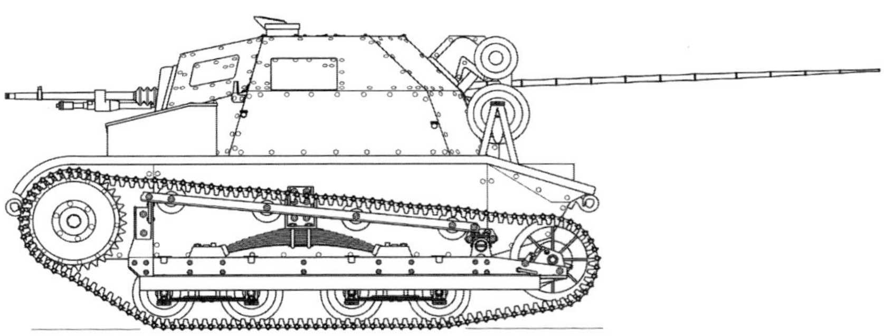

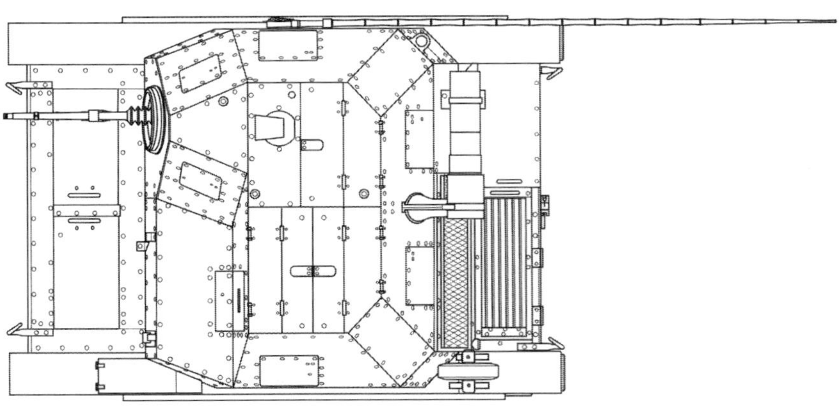

TKS tankette with radio station (left and top view, antenna mast laid 'to march', external prop box and widening caps added, rebuilt rear).

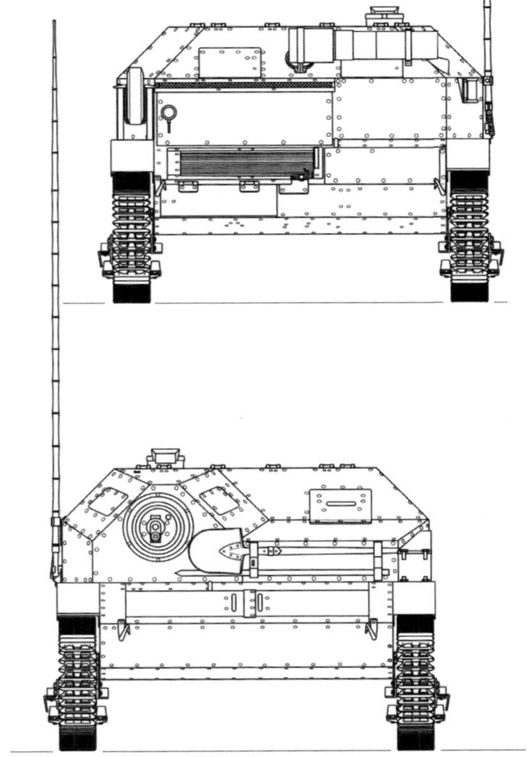

TKS tankette with radio station (front view, mast antenew erected).

1/35

Drawings: Adam Jońca

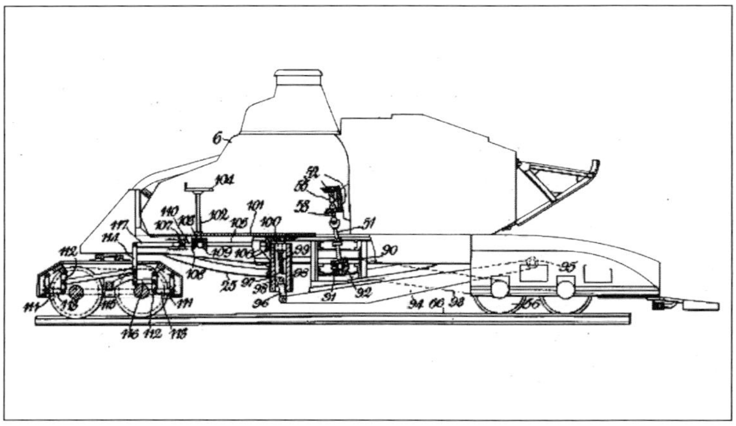

Railway autotransporter for the Renault FT tank – drawing by Tadeusz Kossakowski for an American patent. It was a kind of rail car with a tank – by means of an added gearbox, an intermediate shaft and a drive bridge on the rear axle, the tank could drive itself using its own engine.

Renault tank autotransporter built in the workshops of the 1st Armoured Train Squadron. The drive to the railway road wheels was realised without interfering with the tank structure – a roller assembly transferred the drive to the railway wheels directly from the tank tracks to the wheel chain transmission.

Final form of autotransporter R.

Two drawings from a patent filed in the USA. This is a wagon, keeping a tankette on the track, moving on its own tracks.

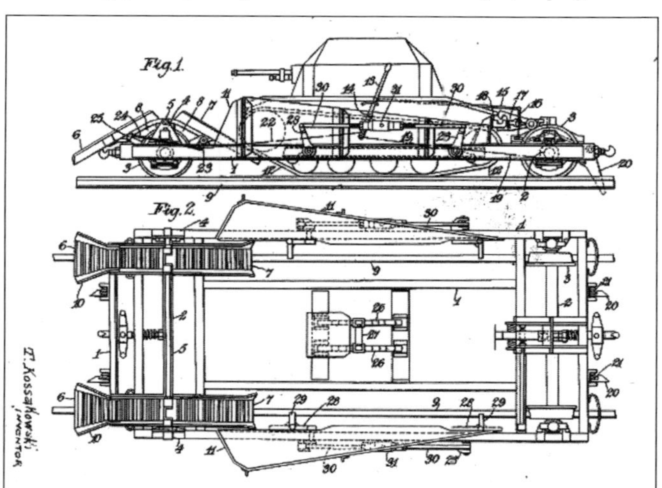

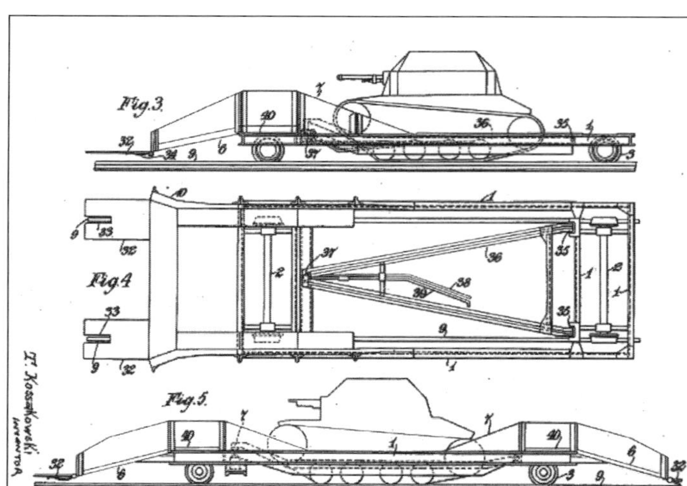

The communications platoon of the 1st Armoured Train Squadron – a photograph of the platoon's soldiers against the background of the artillery car of the armoured train "Danuta". The TK-3 tankette and the TKS tankette were important attributes of the communication platoon – the training of telephone and radio operators was extremely important as the tankettes performed reconnaissance functions and the tasks of advanced fire control posts of the armoured trains.

TK rail track guide with TKS tank, early construction.

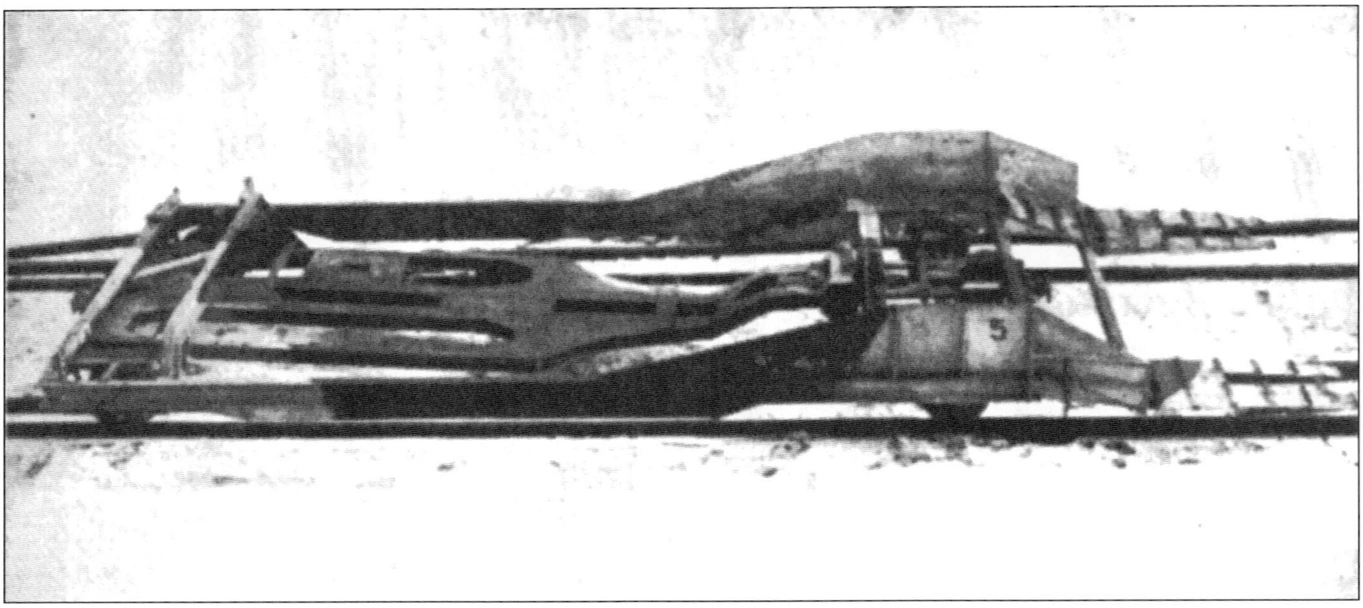

CT rail track guide – photo from "Armoured Weapons Regulations. Description and instructions for the operation of an armoured train". Warsaw 1938.

Photo of one of the early TK rail track guides with a 'radio-controlled' TK-3 tankette (1935, Polish armoured equipment show in Romania).

Technical drawing of an early version of the TK rail track guide.

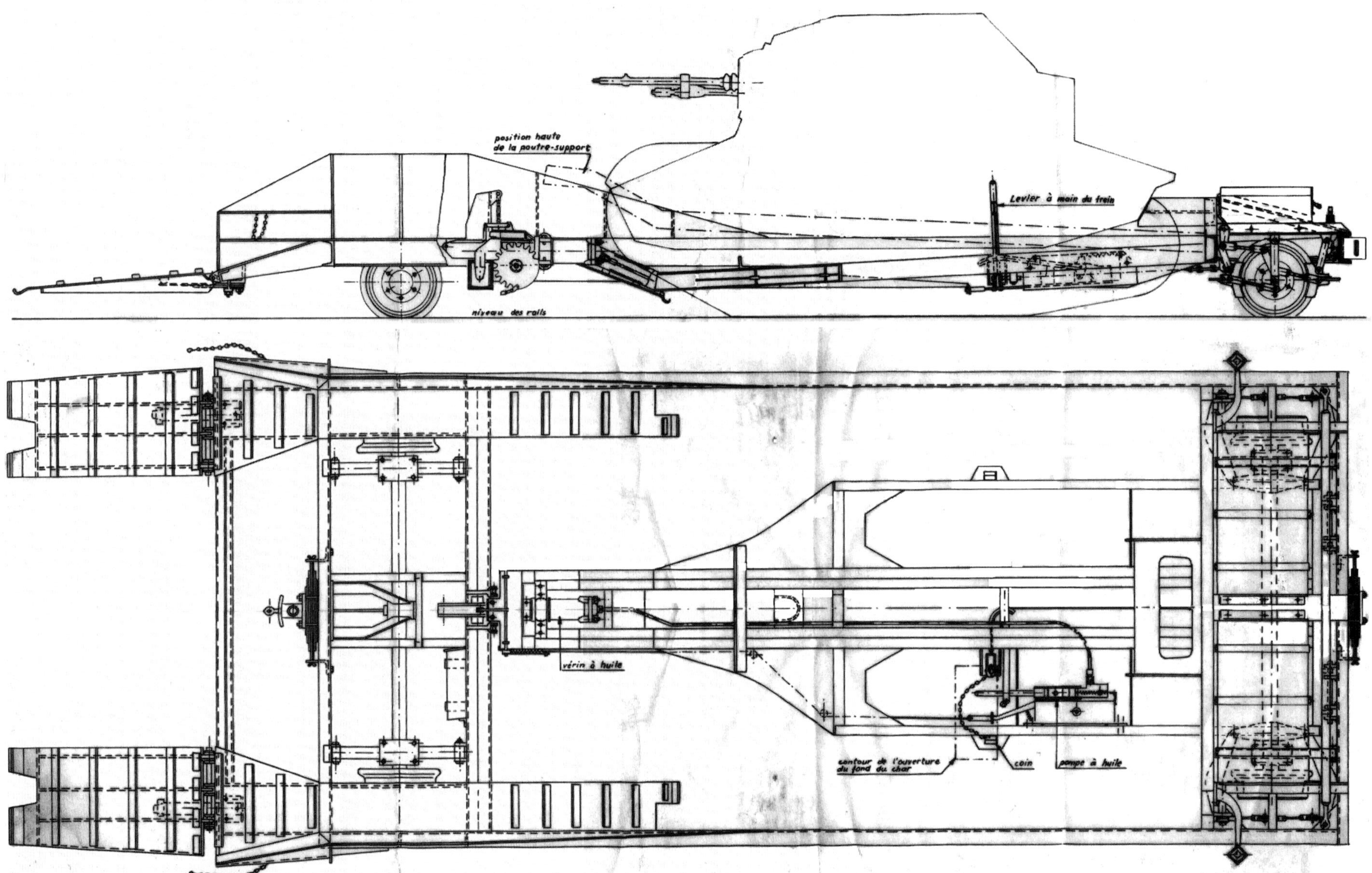

In both pictures the same rail track guide. At the top of the page, a TK draisine with a TK-3 tank. The tank in the process of being adapted for the installation of an RKB/c (Battalion Correspondence/Tank Radio Station) radio station. At the front, on the wing, a requisition box, moved to the rear of the ckm yoke for p.a. firing. Without the requisition box on the rail track guide (more accurately two boxes with a common lid).

Technical drawing of the CT rail track guide way frame. This and subsequent drawings are taken from the "Armoured Train Regulations. Description and instructions for the operation of the rail rail track guide of the tank "T.K. Part II – Atlas", Warsaw 1936.

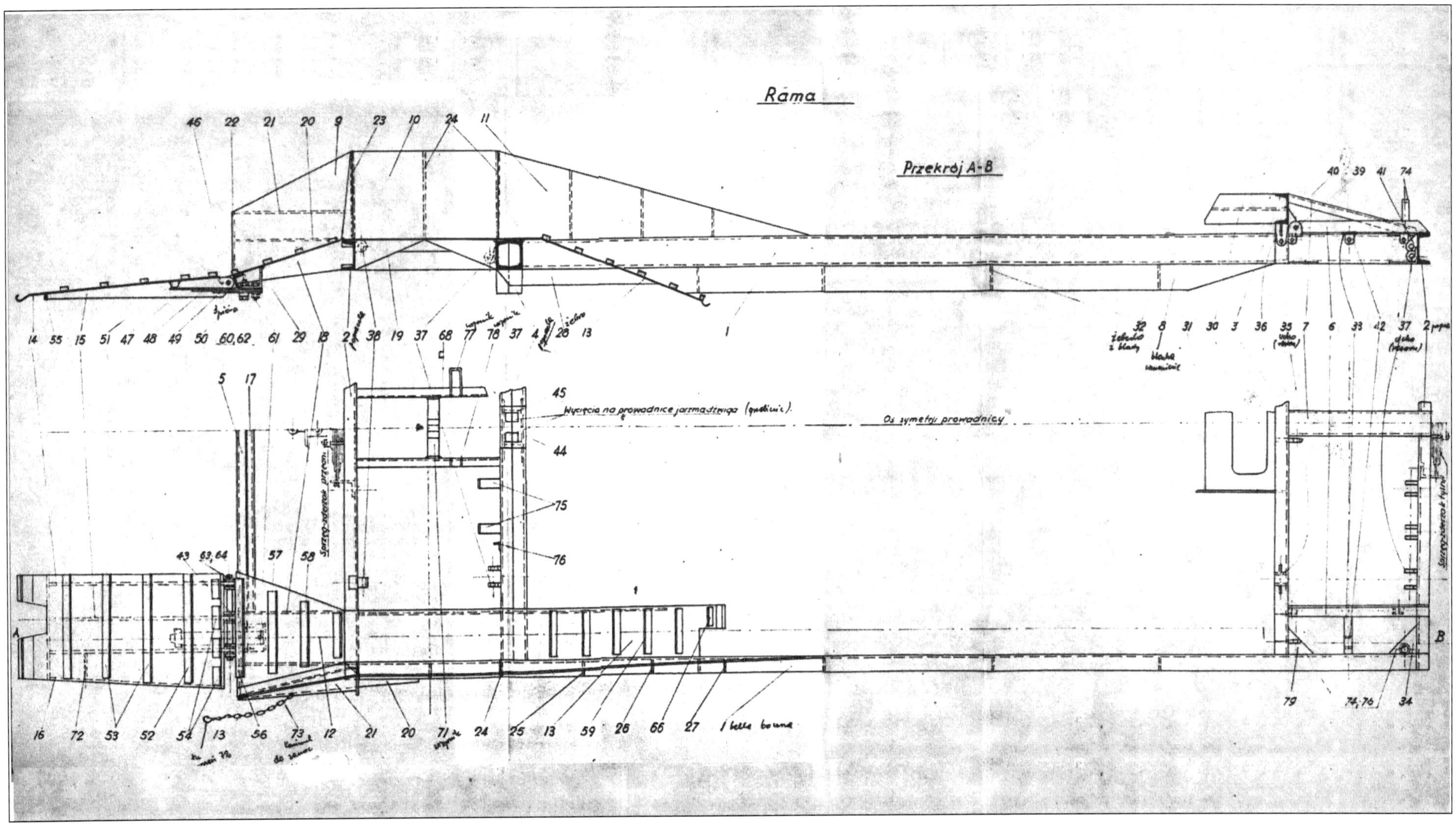

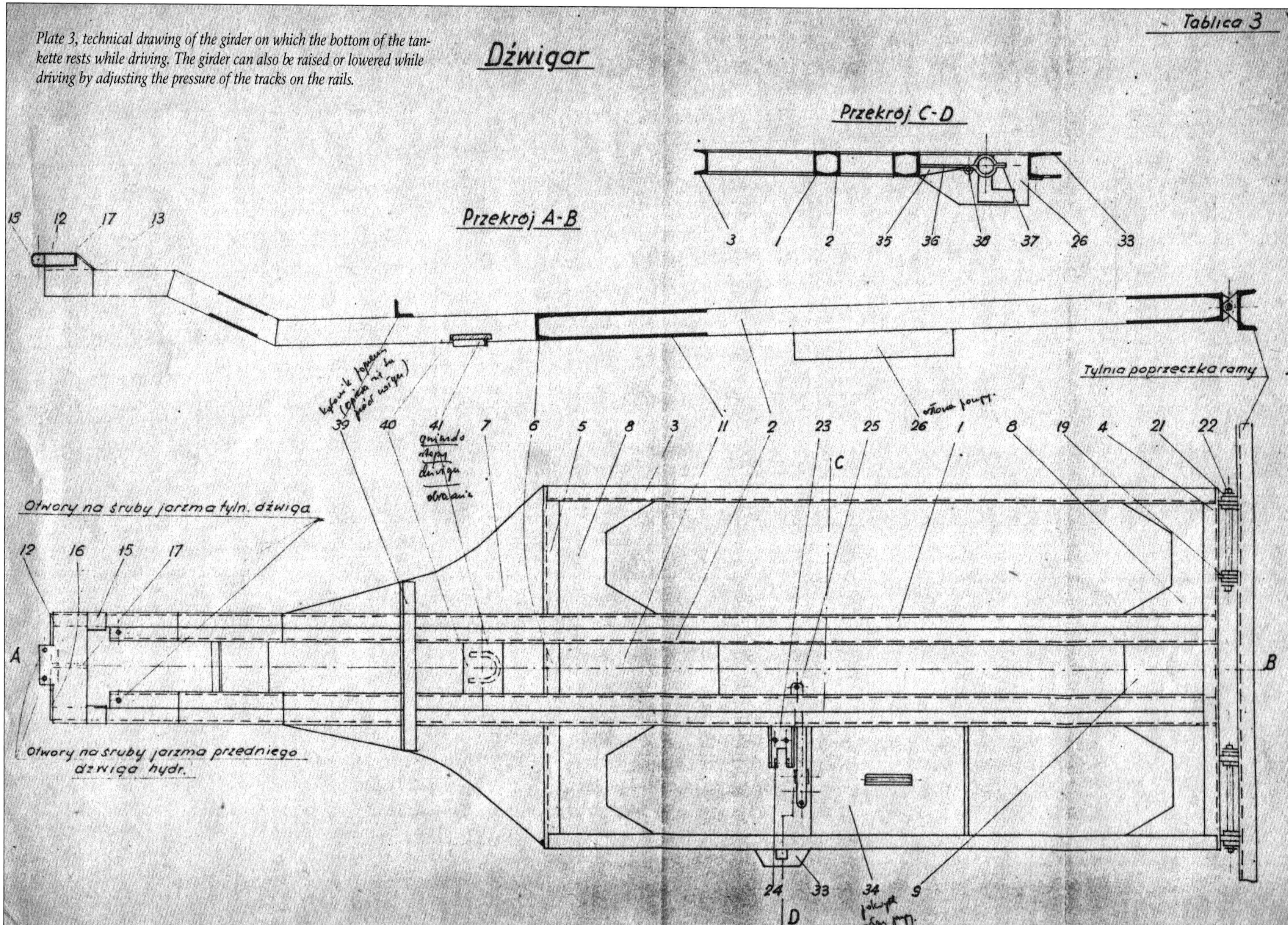

Plate 3, technical drawing of the girder on which the bottom of the tankette rests while driving. The girder can also be raised or lowered while driving by adjusting the pressure of the tracks on the rails.

A visit by Estonian military officers to Legionowo, 1st Armoured Train Squadron. The TK guidon and the R guidon are presented.

TK-3 tanks on guides coupled to R autotransporter.

Technical drawing of girder lifting mechanism (crane) – oil crane.

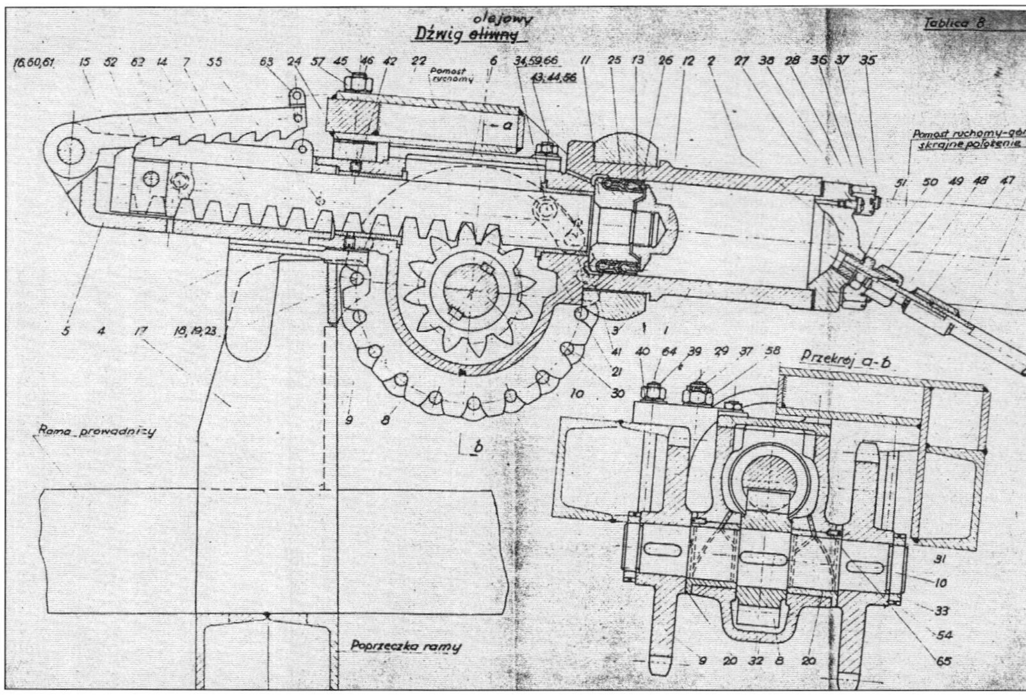

Photo of girder lifting mechanism – girder in upper position.

Photo of the girder lifting mechanism – the girder in the lower position.

View of the front part of the girder with the lifting mechanism.

Control mechanism for the latch that locks the girder in the desired position.

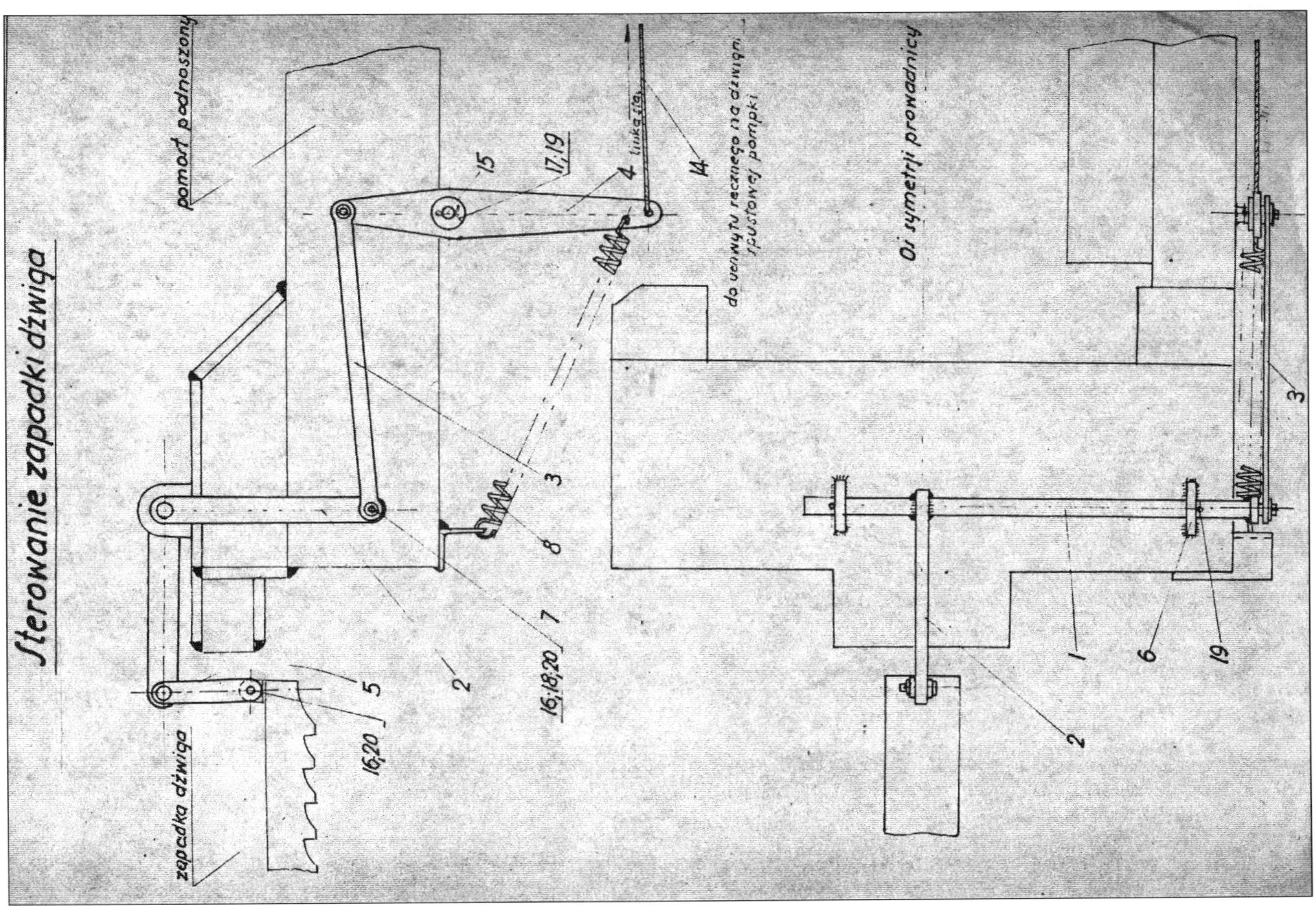

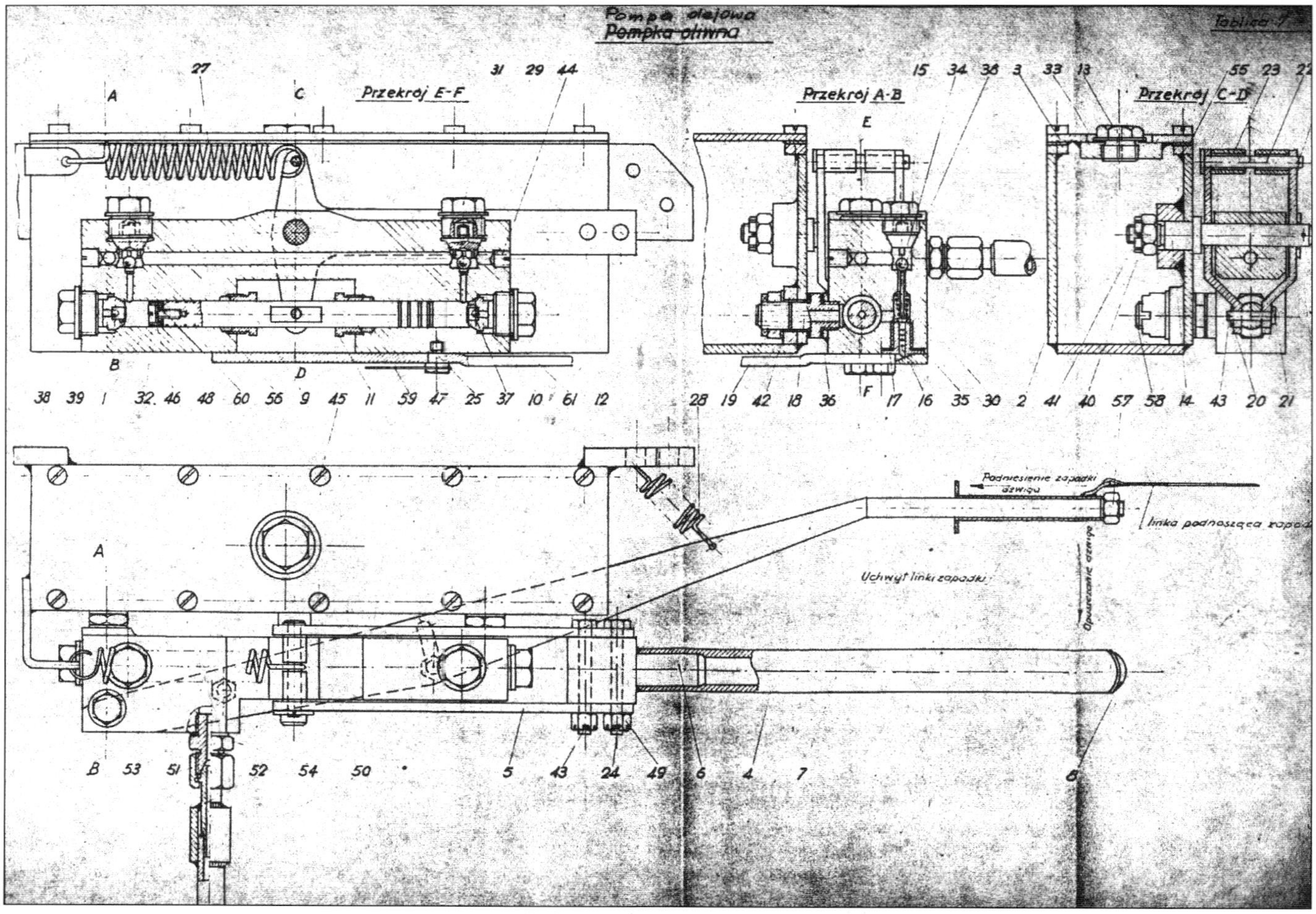

Technical drawing and photograph of the oil pump. The pump is controlled from inside the tank through a vent punch in the bottom of the tank.

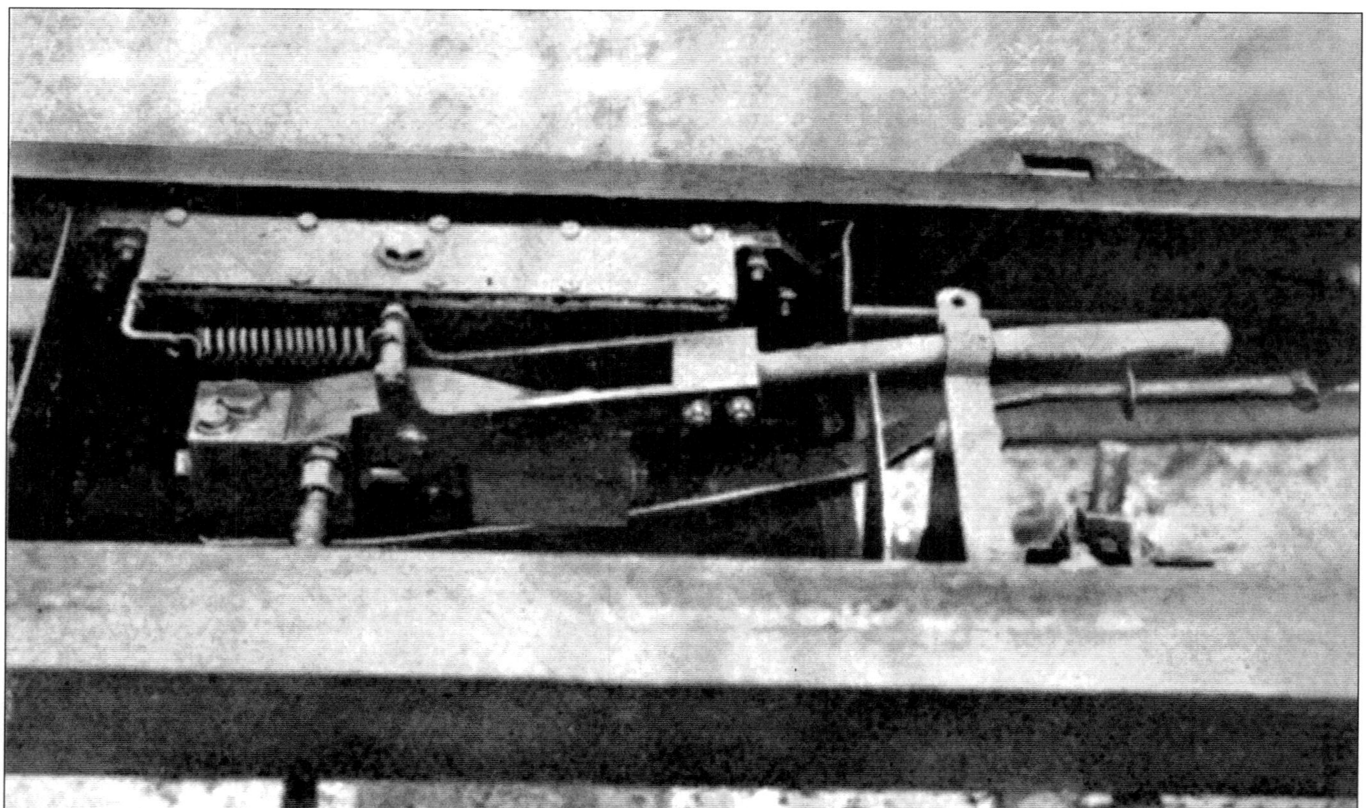

Czerwony Bór station – section of railway line where armoured trains practised. On the shunting track, a TK-R-TK unit covered with tarpaulin sheets.

Romanian army officers looking at the TK-3 radio-controlled tankette. An interesting detail is that the TK-3 tankette is equipped with reversible periscopes. The periscopes significantly improved observation from the tank. Reports recommended embedding periscopes in all tankettes, but this was not realised until the outbreak of war.

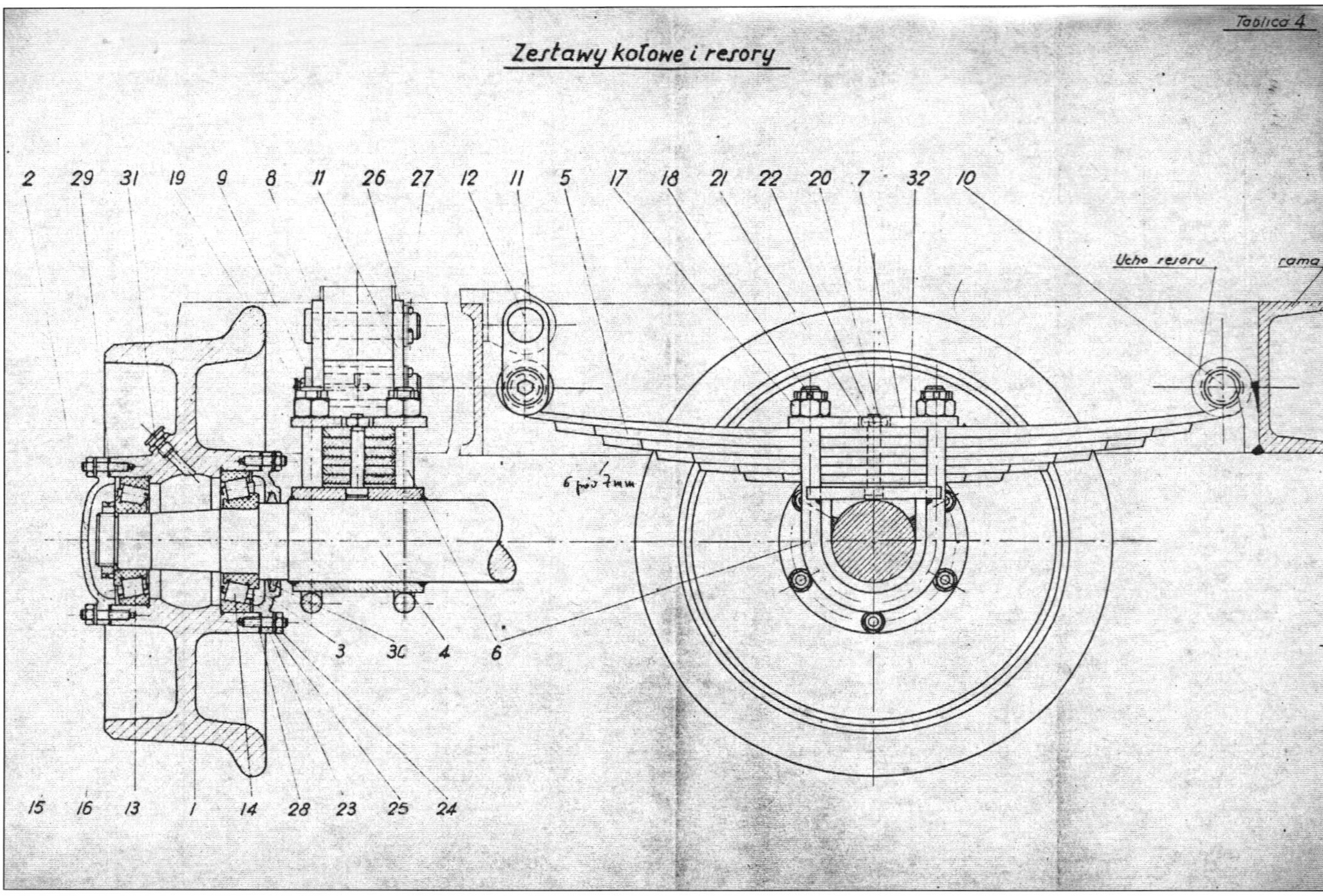

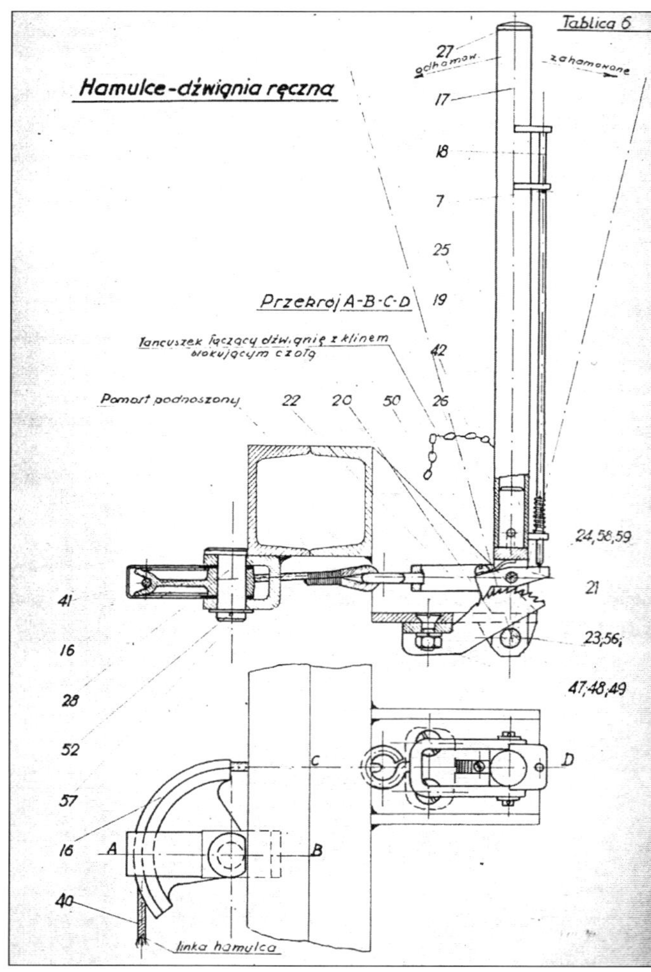

Technical drawing and photo of the wheelset. There were two versions of bearings, initially heavier and two slightly different ways of attaching the springs. Cast wheels with a diameter of 320 mm.

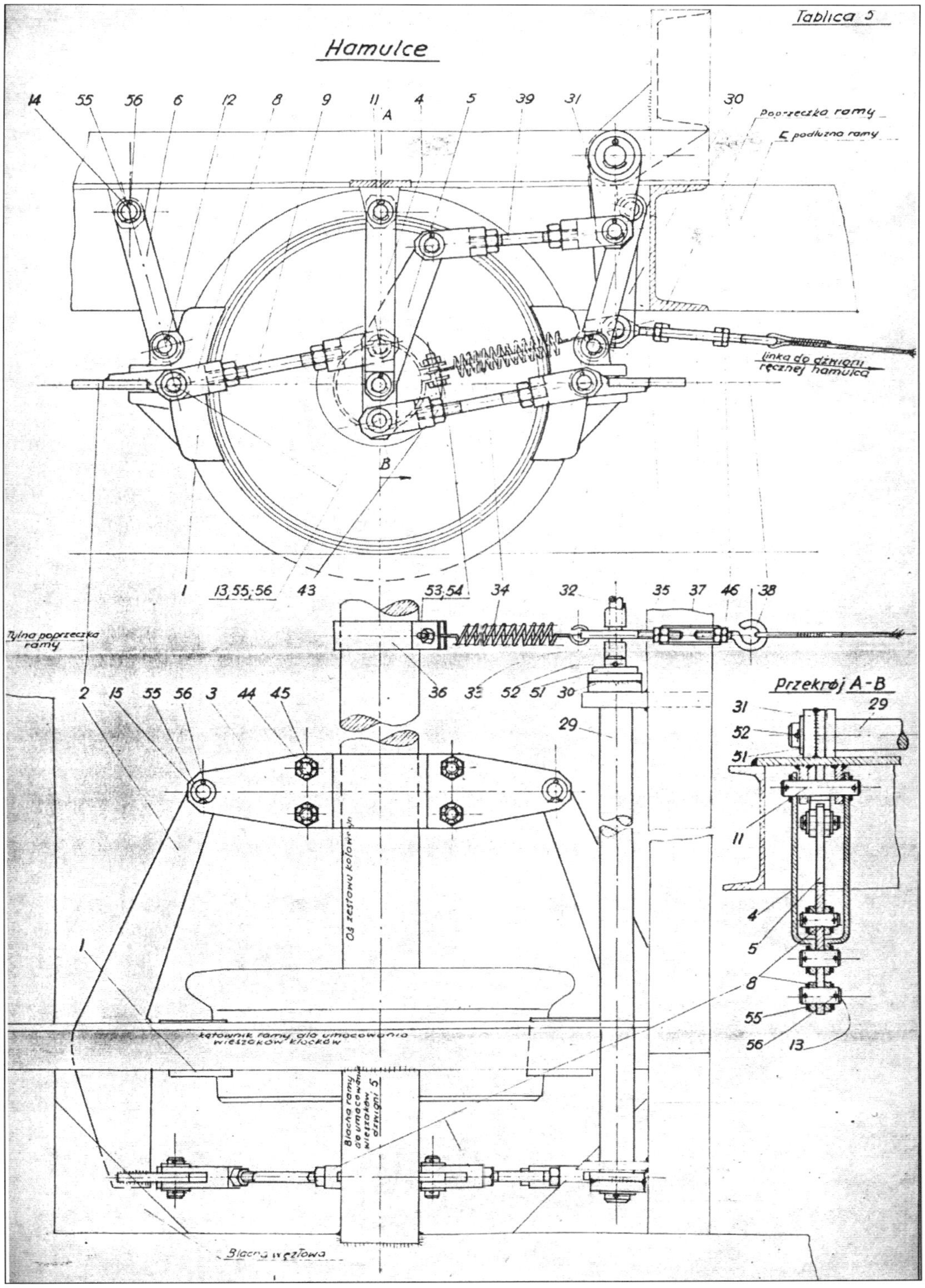

Braking system components.

Brake system components – to the right and left of the rail track guide.

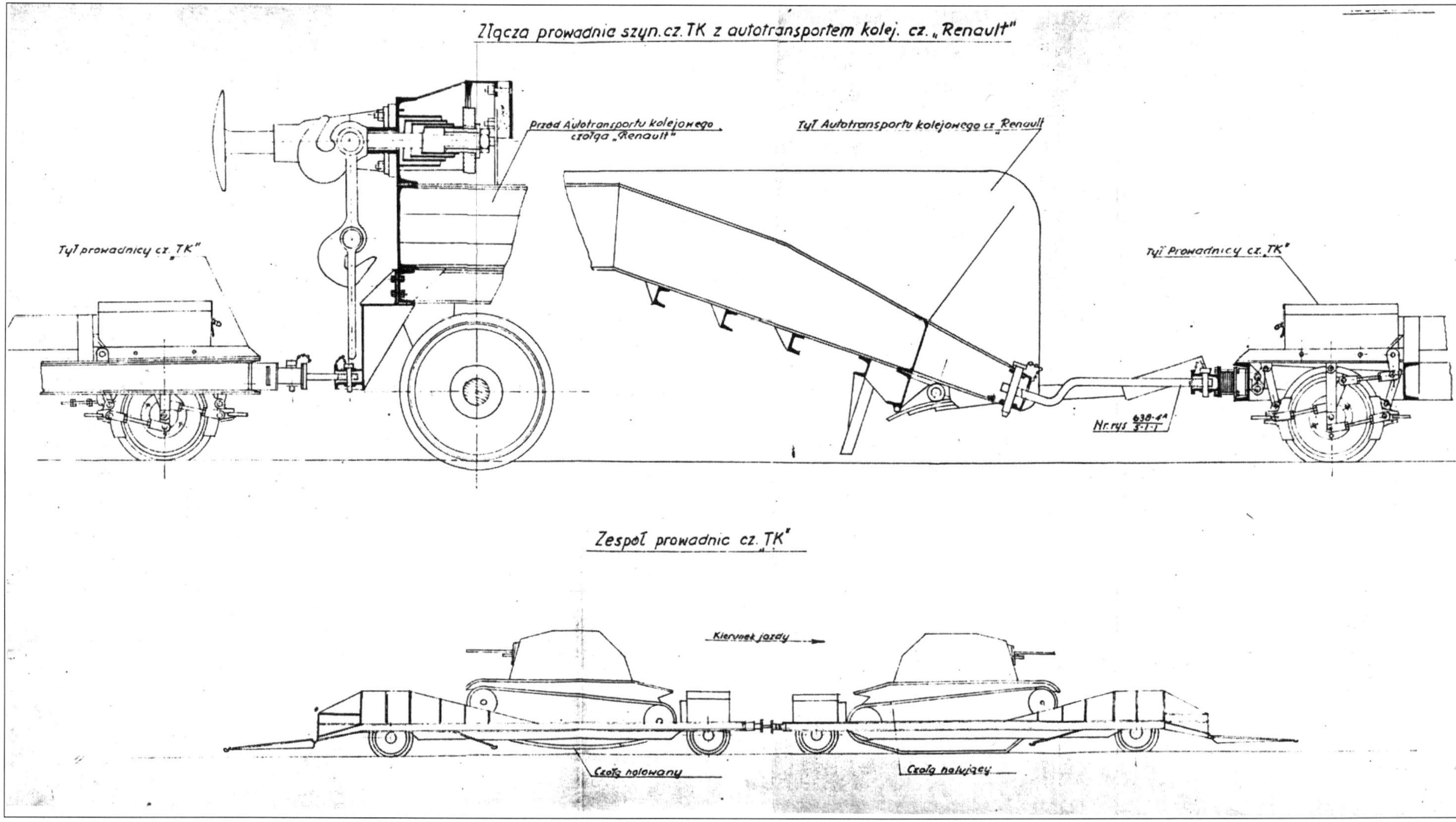

Coupling tankettes with R autotransporter and TK draisine with each other.

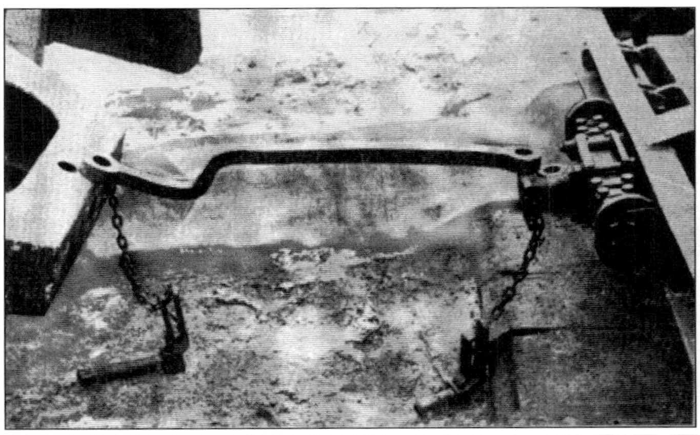

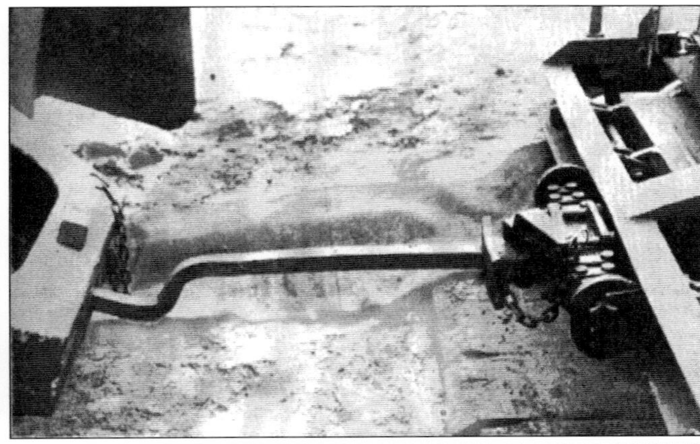

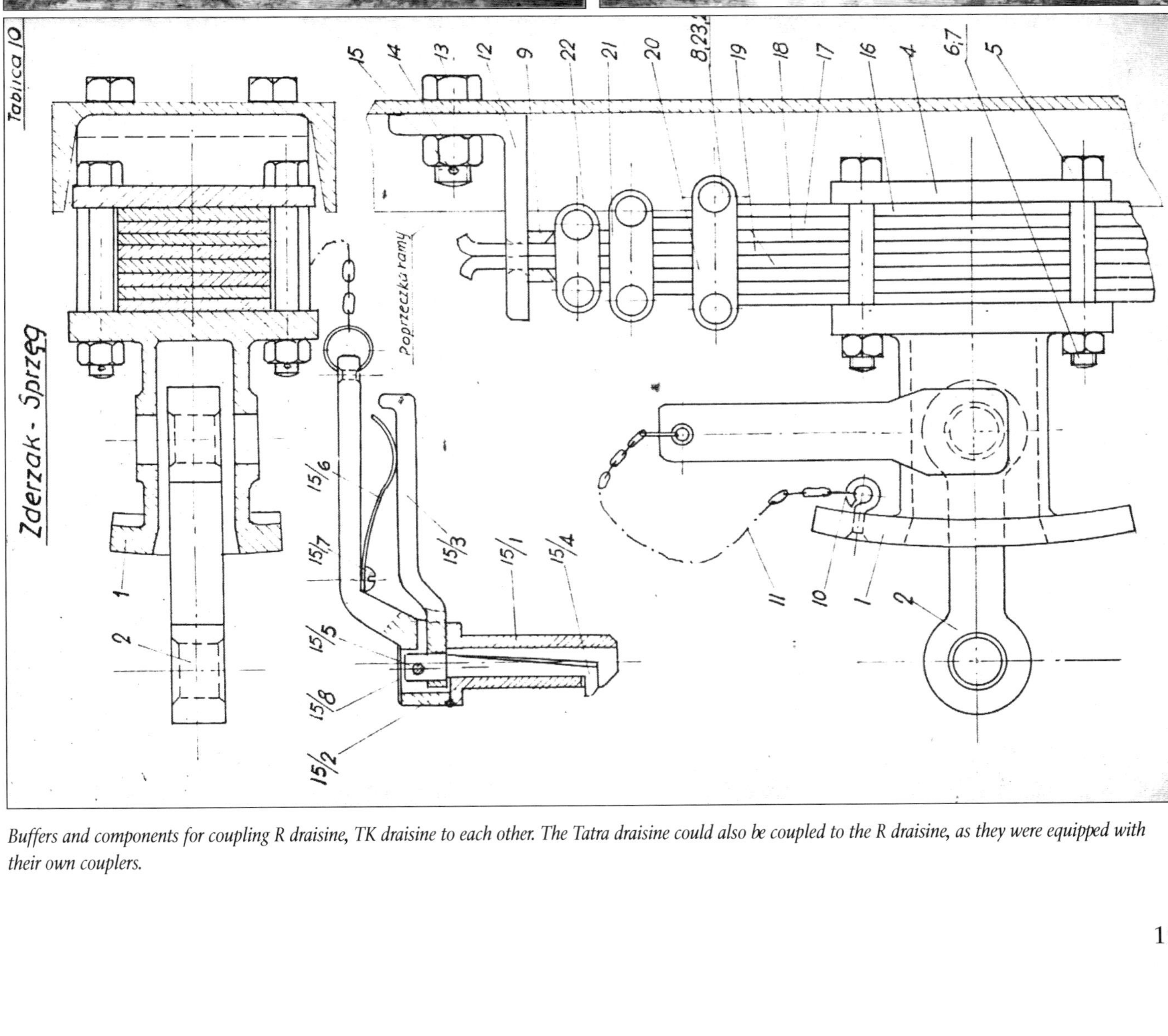

Buffers and components for coupling R draisine, TK draisine to each other. The Tatra draisine could also be coupled to the R draisine, as they were equipped with their own couplers.

Hydraulic lift – once the rail track guide was supported in the centre of gravity, it was possible to rotate the rail track guide with the tankette thus changing the direction of travel 'forward'. Driving in reverse was too slow.

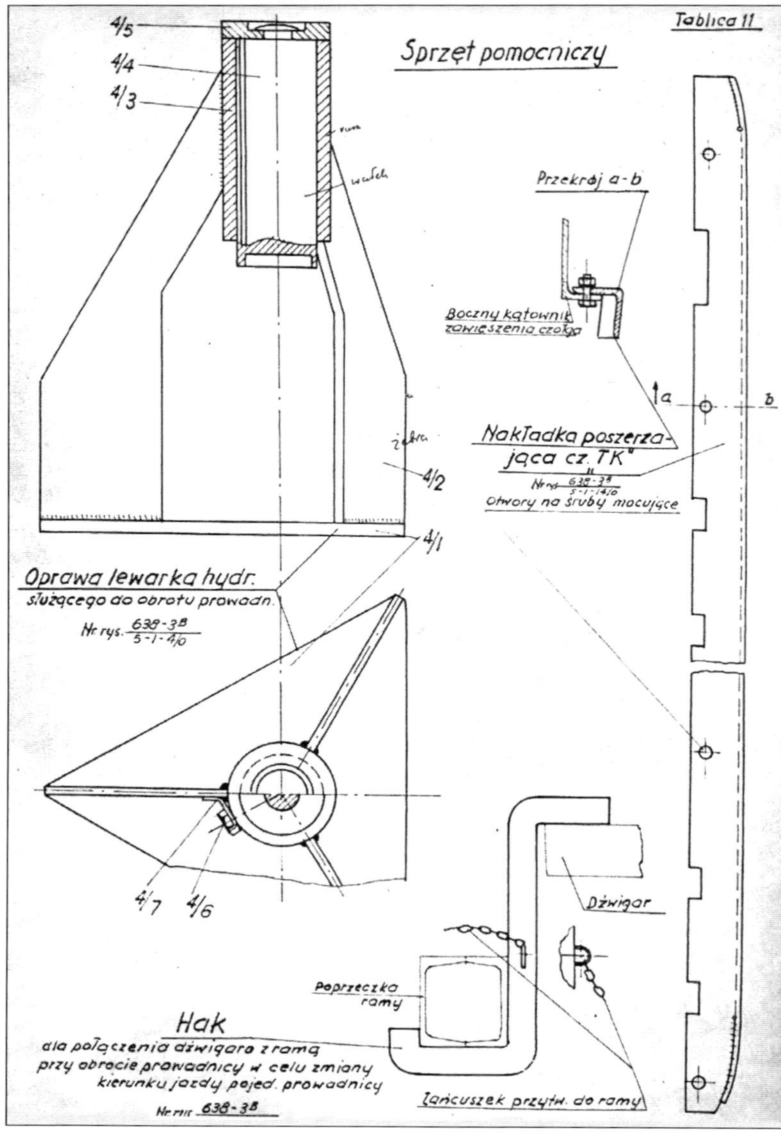

Table 11– ancillary equipment. Widening overlay as recommended, but in practice catered for in various ways.

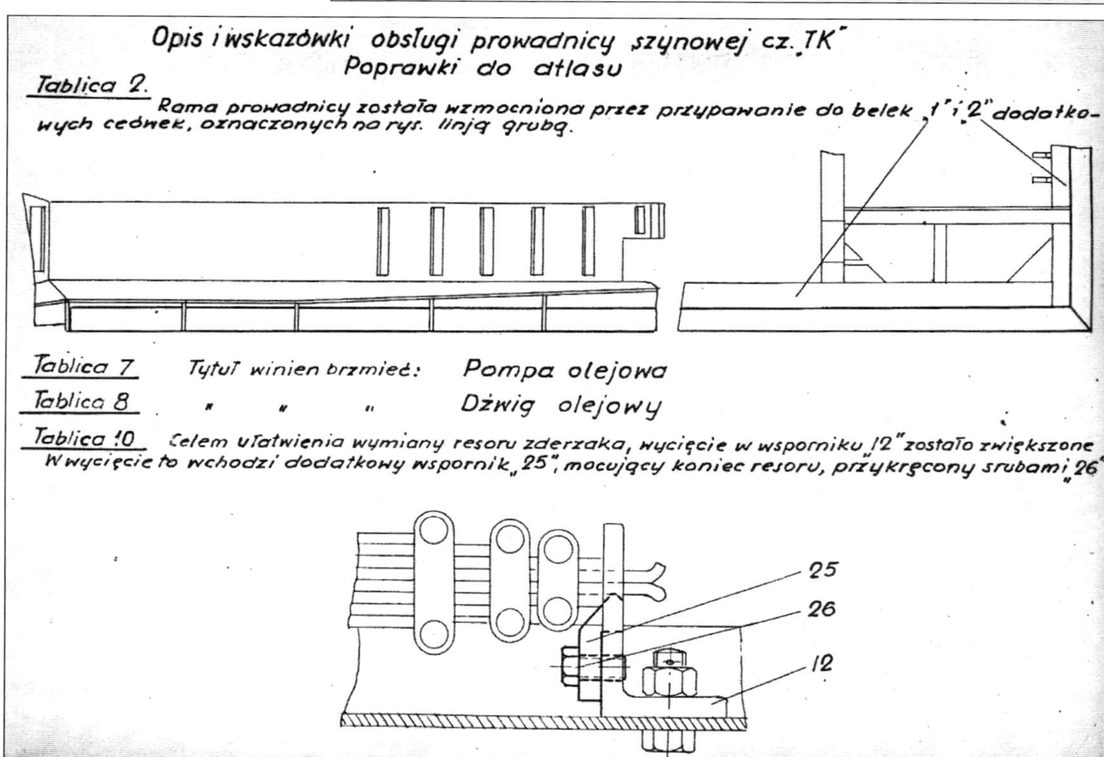

Opis i wskazówki obsługi prowadnicy szynowej cz. „TK"

Poprawki do atlasu

Tablica 2. Rama prowadnicy została wzmocniona przez przypawanie do belek „1" i „2" dodatkowych ceówek, oznaczonych na rys. linją grubą.

Tablica 7 Tytuł winien brzmieć: Pompa olejowa

Tablica 8 " " " Dźwig olejowy

Tablica 10 Celem ułatwienia wymiany resoru zderzaka, wycięcie w wsporniku „12" zostało zwiększone. W wycięcie to wchodzi dodatkowy wspornik „25", mocujący koniec resoru, przykręcony śrubami „26"

The final board in this set – amendments and additions. An important change is the addition of channels to reinforce and stiffen the frame. Most of the rail track guides have been reworked in this way – but not all.

A TK-R-TK assembly with TK-3 tankettes. The tankette has an aerial mast, but no prop boxes or extension cap. The photo was probably taken in 1935.

TK-R-TK assembly with a TK-3 radio tankette. The R draisine is equipped with a radio station, which is located in a tin radio cab located on the entrance ramp. The least two R-trucks were equipped in this way.

A TK-3 tankette with radio station at a demonstration in Romania in 1935.

TK-3 tankette with radio station – prop boxes installed, but undercarriage not was widened with overlays.

TK-3 tankette with radio station – mast laid down and supported by a yoke mount for anti-aircraft firing. Some tankettes had this yoke moved to the slanted rear armour wall and embedded 'forks', with the mast supported by an angle brace.

September 1939. An assembly of draisines of the armoured train "Poznańczyk" (P.P.12)

September 1939, an abandoned TK-R-TK unit of the armoured train "Danuta" (i.e. P.P.11). What happened to the tankettes we do not know. It is worth noting that the rail track guide frames were not reinforced.

September 1939. An assembly of draisines of the armoured train "Poznańczyk" (P.P.12).

September 1939. The armoured train "Poznańczyk" and a whole platoon of draisine after rolling to the collecting station of the German war capture in Sochaczew.

The draisine platoon of the armoured train "General Sosnkowski" (P.P.13) was sent before the war to reinforce the defence of the bridge in Tczew. The photos show the platoon's rolling stock abandoned during the retreat.

Near Żabinka, the tankettes of the "Bartosz Głowacki" train (P.P.55) came off the rails and engaged in combat with a German armoured drive. All were lost, but fortunately their crews managed to return to the train without loss.

German wartime capture – we do not know the remains of which platoon of draisine was loaded onto the platforms.

Pictured is a model of a TKS rail track guide way and tankette. The model, built in 1:35 scale, was made by Jarosław Kieliszek – he used drawings and photographs presented in this Single Vehicle booklet. The model is now in the Historical Museum in Legionowo, in the 'Piaski' branch, in a restored former military casino.

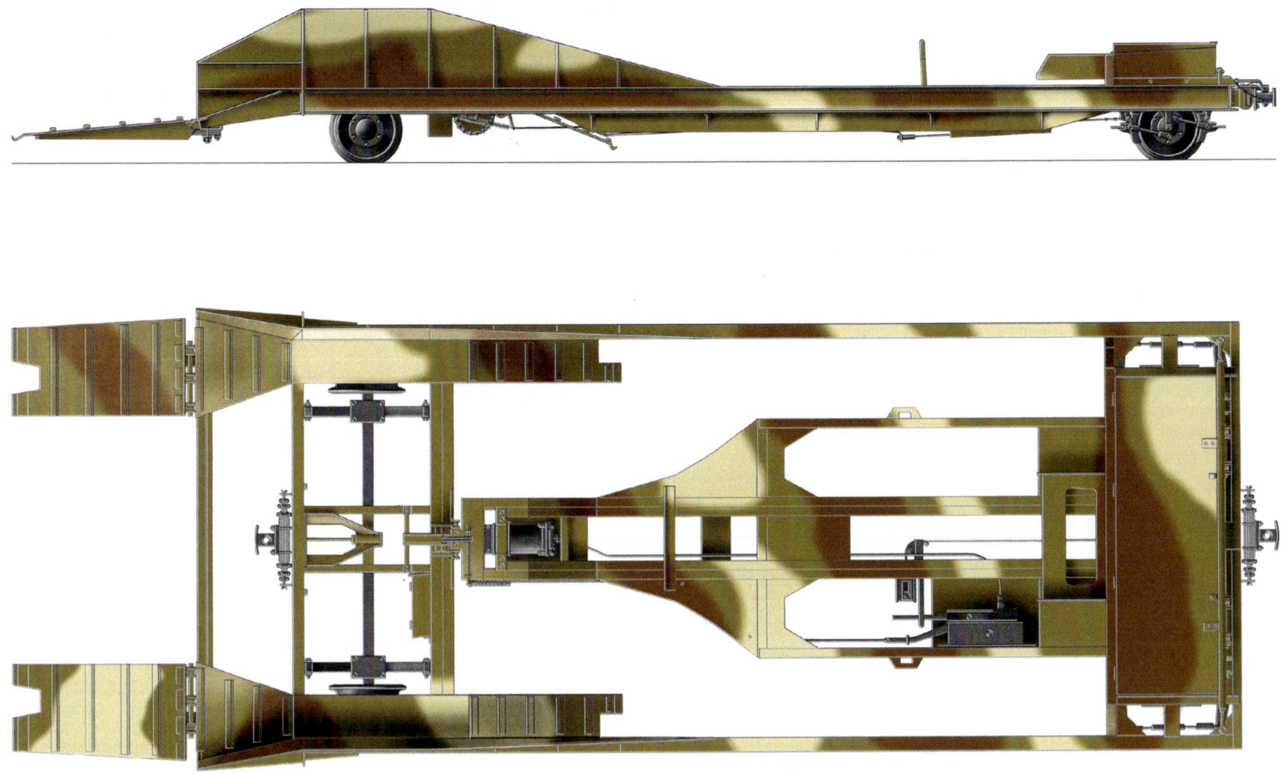

TK rail track guide in side and top view.

TK-3 tankette with radio station.

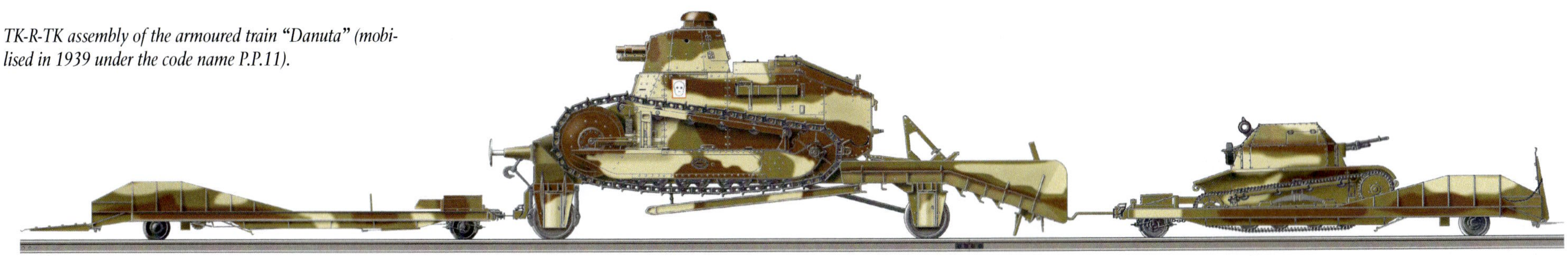

TK-R-TK assembly of the armoured train "Danuta" (mobilised in 1939 under the code name P.P.11).